In the Year 1952

By

Kerry Butters.

In the Year 1952

Millennium: 2nd millennium

Centuries: 19th century – **20th century** – 21st century

Decades: 1920s 1930s 1940s – **1950s** – 1960s 1970s 1980s

Years: 1949 1950 1951 – **1952** – 1953 1954 1955

1952 (MCMLII) was a leap year starting on Tuesday (dominical letter FE) of the Gregorian calendar, the 1952nd year of the Common Era (CE) and *Anno Domini* (AD) designations, the 952nd year of the 2nd millennium, the 52nd year of the 20th century, and the 3rd year of the 1950s decade.

Contents

Events

January

- January 8 – West Germany has 8 million refugees inside its borders.
- January 12 – The University of Tennessee admits its first black student.

February

- February 2 – A tropical storm forms just north of Cuba moving northeast. The storm makes landfall in southern Florida the next day. It is the earliest reported landfall from a tropical storm, and the earliest formation of a tropical storm on record in the Atlantic basin.
- February 6
    - George VI (King of the United Kingdom and the Dominions: Canada, Australia, New Zealand, South Africa, Pakistan and Ceylon) dies aged 56 after a long illness. He is succeeded by his daughter The Princess Elizabeth, Duchess of Edinburgh (now Elizabeth II), who is on a visit to Kenya. She is proclaimed Queen of Canada at Rideau Hall, Ottawa.

- In the United States, a mechanical heart is used for the first time in a human patient.
- February 7 – Elizabeth II is proclaimed Queen of the United Kingdom at St James's Palace, London, England.
- February 14 – February 25 – The Winter Olympics held in Oslo, Norway.
- February 15 – The funeral of George VI takes place at St George's Chapel, Windsor Castle.
- February 18 – Greece and Turkey join the North Atlantic Treaty Organization.
- February 20
  - Emmett Ashford becomes the first African-American umpire in organized baseball, by being authorized to be a substitute umpire in the Southwestern International League.
  - Winston Churchill scraps UK compulsory national identity cards.
- February 21 – In Dhaka, East Pakistan (present-day Bangladesh) police open fire on a procession of students, killing 4 people and starting a country-wide protest which leads to the recognition of Bengali as one of the national languages of Pakistan. The day is later declared "International Mother Language Day" by UNESCO.
- February 25 – The Parícutin active volcano in Michoacán, west central Mexico, ceases its discontinuous eruption after spewing forth a gigaton of lava and burying San Juan Parangaricutiro.
- February 26
  - United Kingdom Prime Minister Winston Churchill announces that the United Kingdom has an atomic bomb.

- Vincent Massey is sworn in as the first Canada-born Governor General of Canada.

March

- March 10 – General Fulgencio Batista re-takes power in Cuba.
- March 15–16 – 73 inches (1,870 mm) of rain falls in Cilaos, Réunion, the most rainfall in one day up to that time.
- March 20 – The United States Senate ratifies a peace treaty with Japan.
- March 21
  - The last two executions in the Netherlands take place.
  - Dr. Kwame Nkrumah is elected Prime Minister of the Gold Coast.
  - Tornadoes ravage the lower Mississippi River Valley, leaving 208 dead, through March 22.
- March 22 – Wernher von Braun publishes the first in his series of articles titled *Man Will Conquer Space Soon!*, including ideas for manned flights to Mars and the Moon.
- March 27 – Konrad Adenauer survives an assassination attempt.
- March 29 – U.S. President Harry S. Truman announces that he will not seek reelection.

April

- April 4
  - In the Hague Tribunal, Israel demands reparations worth $3 billion from Germany.

- West Ice accidents: During a severe storm in the West Ice, east of Greenland, 78 seal hunters on 5 Norwegian seal hunting vessels vanish without a trace.
- April 7 – The American Research Bureau reports that the *I Love Lucy* episode, "The Marriage License" was the first TV show in history to be seen in around 10,000,000 homes the evening the episode aired.
- April 8 – *Youngstown Sheet & Tube Co. v. Sawyer*: The U.S. Supreme Court limits the power of the President to seize private business, after President Harry S. Truman nationalizes all steel mills in the United States, just before the 1952 steel strike begins.
- April 9 – Hugo Ballivián's government is overthrown by the Bolivian National Revolution, which starts a period of agrarian reform, universal suffrage and the nationalization of tin mines.
- April 11 – Battle of Nanri Island: The Republic of China seizes the island from the Peoples' Republic of China.
- April 15 – The United States B-52 Stratofortress flies for the first time.
- April 18
  - Bolivia National Revolution: A universal vote enables indigenous peoples and women to vote, nationalizes mines and enacts agrarian reform.
  - West Germany and Japan form diplomatic relations.
- April 26 – The United States Navy aircraft carrier *Wasp* collides with the destroyer *Hobson* while on exercises in the Atlantic Ocean, killing 175 men.
- April 28 – The Treaty of San Francisco goes into effect, formally ending the war between Japan and the Allies, and simultaneously ending the occupation of the four main

Japanese islands by the Supreme Commander for the Allied Powers.

- April 29 – Lever House officially opens at 390 Park Avenue in New York City, heralding a new age of commercial architecture in the United States. Designed by Gordon Bunshaft of Skidmore, Owings & Merrill, it is the first International Style skyscraper.

May

- May 1 – East Germany threatens to form its own army.
- May 2 – The first passenger jet flight route opens between London and Johannesburg.
- May 3 – U.S. lieutenant colonels Joseph O. Fletcher and William P. Benedict land a plane at the geographic North Pole.
- May 6 – Farouk of Egypt has himself announced as a descendant of the Islamic prophet, Muhammad.
- May 13 – Pandit Nehru forms his first government in India.
- May 15 – Diplomatic relations are established between Israel and Japan at the level of legations.
- May 18 – Ann Davison becomes the first woman to single-handedly sail the Atlantic Ocean.

June

- June 1
  - The Roman Catholic Church bans the books of André Gide.
  - Navigation opens on the Volga–Don Canal, connecting the Caspian Sea basin with that of the Black Sea.
  -

- June 14
  - The keel is laid for the U.S. nuclear submarine USS *Nautilus*.
  - Myxomatosis is introduced to Europe on the French estate of Dr. Paul-Félix Armand-Delille.
- June 15 – *The Diary of a Young Girl* is published.
- June 19 – The Special Forces (United States Army) are created.
- June 21 – The Philippine School of Commerce, through a government act, is converted to the Philippine College of Commerce (later the Polytechnic University of the Philippines).
- June 26 – The Pan-Malayan Labour Party is founded in Malaya, as a union of statewise labour parties.
- June 27 – Decree 900 in Guatemala orders redistribution of uncultivated land.
- June 29 – Finnish contestant Armi Kuusela wins the title of Miss Universe.

July

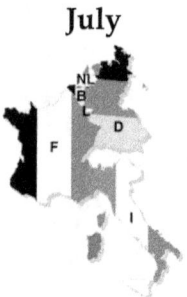

France, West Germany, Italy, Belgium, Luxembourg and the Netherlands form the European Coal and Steel community, the foundation organization which would become the European Union.

- July 3 – The ocean liner SS *United States* makes her maiden crossing of the Atlantic.
- July 13 – East Germany announces the formation of its National People's Army.
- July 19 – August 3 – The 1952 Summer Olympics are held in Helsinki, Finland.
- July 21 – The 7.3 Mw Kern County earthquake strikes Southern California with a maximum Mercalli intensity of XI (*Extreme*), killing 12 and injuring hundreds.
- July 23
    - The European Coal and Steel Community is established.
    - General Mohammed Naguib leads The Free Officers (formed by Gamal Abdel Nasser – the real power behind the coup) in the overthrow of King Farouk of Egypt.
- July 25 – Puerto Rico becomes a self-governing commonwealth of the United States.

August

- August 5 – The Treaty of Taipei between Japan and the Republic of China goes into effect, to officially end the Second Sino-Japanese War.
- August 11 – The Jordanian Parliament forces King Talal of Jordan to abdicate due to mental illness; he is succeeded by his son King Hussein.
- August 12 – The Night of the Murdered Poets; the execution of 13 Soviet Jewish poets.
- August 13 – Japan joins the IMF.
- August 14 – West Germany joins the IMF and the World Bank.

- August 16 – Lynmouth, North Devon, England is devastated by floods; 34 die.
- August 26 – A British passenger jet makes a return crossing of the Atlantic Ocean in the same day.
- August 27 – Reparation negotiations between West Germany and Israel end in Luxembourg: Germany will pay 3 billion Deutsche Marks.
- August 29 – Composer John Cage's 4'33", during which the performer does not play, premieres in Woodstock, New York.
- August 30 – The last Finnish war reparations are sent to the Soviet Union.
- August 31 – The Grenzlandring racetrack closes in Wegberg, Germany.

September

- September 2 – Dr. C. Walton Lillehei and Dr. F. John Lewis perform the first open-heart surgery at the University of Minnesota.
- September 6 – Television debuts in Canada as the CBC in Montreal, Quebec airs.
- September 8 – CBC Toronto debuts.
- September 10 – The European Parliamentary Assembly (from March 1962, European Parliament) opens.
- September 18 – The Soviet Union vetoes Japan's application for membership in the United Nations.
- September 30 – The Revised Standard Version of the Bible was published and released to the public.

October

- October 3 – The first British nuclear weapon is detonated in Australia making the United Kingdom the third nuclear weapons state.
- October 8
  - Negotiations for a ceasefire in Korea are postponed.
  - Harrow and Wealdstone rail crash in England kills 112 people.
- October 12 – The Gamma Sigma Sigma National Service Sorority is founded in New York City at Panhellenic Tower.
- October 14 – The United Nations begins work in the new United Nations building in New York City, designed by Le Corbusier and Oscar Niemeyer.
- October 16 – *Limelight* opens in London; writer/actor/director/producer Charlie Chaplin arrives by ocean liner; in transit his re-entry permit to the USA is revoked by J. Edgar Hoover.
- October 17 – Indonesian troops led by General Nasution surround the presidential palace, seeking the dismissal of the People's Representative Council; Sukarno avoids confrontation.
- October 19
  - Alain Bombard begins to sail from the Canary Islands to Barbados in 65 days; he reaches them December 23.
  - John Bamford, aged 15, rescues victims of a house fire and becomes the youngest person to be awarded the George Cross.
- October 20 – Martial law is declared in Kenya due to the Mau Mau uprising.

November

- November 1 – Nuclear testing and Operation Ivy: The United States successfully detonates the first hydrogen bomb, codenamed "Mike", at Eniwetok Atoll in the Marshall Islands in the central Pacific Ocean, with a yield of 10.4 megatons.

The explosion of the first hydrogen bomb.

- November 4
  - The Mw 9.0 Severo-Kurilsk earthquake hits the Kamchatka Peninsula of the Soviet Union with a maximum Mercalli intensity of XI (*Extreme*). A tsunami took the lives of more than 2,000 people.
  - United States presidential election, 1952: Republican General Dwight D. Eisenhower defeats Democratic Governor of Illinois Adlai Stevenson (correctly predicted by the UNIVAC computer).
  - The U.S. National Security Agency is founded.
  - The Pace-Finletter MOU 1952: A Memorandum of understanding is signed between "...Air Force Secretary Finletter and Army Secretary Pace that established a fixed wing weight limit [for the Army] of five thousand pounds empty, but weight restrictions on helicopters were eliminated..."

- November 18 – Jomo Kenyatta is arrested in Kenya for an alleged connection to the Mau Mau Uprising.
- November 20
  - Slánský trials: A series of largely anti-Semitic show trials are held in Czechoslovakia.
  - A fireball crashes in a backyard in Havelock North, New Zealand.
  - The first official passenger flight over the North Pole is made from Los Angeles to Copenhagen.
  - The first successful sex reasignment surgery was performed in Copenhagen, making George Jorgensen Jr. become Christine Jorgensen.
- November 25 – Agatha Christie's murder-mystery play *The Mousetrap* opens at the Ambassadors Theatre in London; as of 2015, it continues next door at the St. Martin's Theatre, and remains the longest continuously running production of a play in history.
- November 29 – Korean War: U.S. President-elect Dwight D. Eisenhower fulfills a political campaign promise, by traveling to Korea to find out what can be done to end the conflict.

December

- December 1
  - Adolfo Ruiz Cortines takes office as President of Mexico.
  - The *New York Daily News* carries a front page story announcing that Christine Jorgensen, a transsexual woman in Denmark, has become the recipient of the first successful sexual reassignment operation.

- December 4 – the Great Smog: A "killer fog" descends on London (in the process coining the word "Smog", for "smoke" and "fog").
- December 14 – The first successful surgical separation of Siamese twins is conducted in Mount Sinai Hospital, Cleveland, Ohio.
- December 20 – The crash of a U.S. Air Force C-124 Globemaster at Moses Lake, WA kills 86 servicemen.
- December 25 – One West German soldier is killed in a shooting incident in West Berlin.
- December 26 – Joseph Ivor Linton, the first Israeli Minister Plenipotentiary in Japan, presents his credentials to the Emperor of Japan.

Date unknown

- Nearly 58,000 cases of polio are reported in the U.S.; 3,145 die and 21,269 are left with mild to disabling paralysis.
- The Nordic Council agrees to the unrestricted transport of people, goods and services throughout the Nordic Countries.
- The National Prohibition Foundation is incorporated in Indiana.
- Säynätsalo Town Hall in Finland, designed by Alvar Aalto, is completed.
- The influential multistorey residential building, Unité d'Habitation in Marseille, France, designed by Le Corbusier, is completed.
- The American Embassy School of New Delhi is founded.
- Swedish paratrooper training school Fallskärmsjägarna (FJS) is established.

- Twelve-year-old Jimmy Boyd's record of *I Saw Mommy Kissing Santa Claus* is released, selling 3 million records
- Capitol Wrestling Corporation, the professional wrestling promotion that would later evolve into the modern day WWE is founded by Jess McMahon and Toots Mondt
- During the Mau Mau Uprising, the poisonous latex of the African milk bush was used to kill cattle in an incident of Biological warfare.

Births

January

Park Geun-hye

Tomislav Nikolić

- January 1 – Jury Zacharanka, Belarusian politician
- January 2
  - Makoto Nakajima, Japanese bureaucrat, Commissoner of the Japan Patent Office

- Ng Man-tat, Hong Kong actor
- January 3 – Jim Ross, American wrestling announcer
- January 7 – Sammo Hung, Hong Kong martial arts superstar, producer and director
- January 9 – Marek Belka, Prime Minister of Poland
- January 12
  - Charles Faulkner, American life coach, motivational speaker, trader and author
  - Walter Mosley, American author
- January 14 – Maureen Dowd, American journalist
- January 15 – Boris Blank, Swiss musician
- January 15 – Skay Beilinson, Argentinian guitar player
- January 16 – H.R.H. Prince Ahmed Fuad Farouk (Fuad II), the last King of Egypt & Sudan, Nubia, Kordofan and Darfur
- January 17 – Ryuichi Sakamoto, Japanese musician, composer, producer, and actor (*Yellow Magic Orchestra*)
- January 21
  - Marco Camenisch, Swiss environmental activist
  - Louis Menand, American writer and critic
- January 22 – Ace Vergel, Filipino actor (d. 2007)
- January 24 – Raymond Domenech, French football player and manager
- January 25
  - Edward Fialkowski, Polish political activist
  - Sara Mandiano, French singer and songwriter
  - Peter Tatchell, Australian-born British human rights activist
- January 28 – Tomokazu Miura, Japanese actor
- January 29 – Klaus-Peter Hanisch, German footballer (d. 2009)

- January 31 – Jan Hofer, German journalist, broadcast news analyst and television presenter

February

- February 1 – Stan Kasten, American baseball executive, currently President of the Washington Nationals
- February 2 – Park Geun-hye, President of South Korea
- February 4 – Jenny Shipley, former Prime Minister of New Zealand
- February 7 – Tony Liu, Chinese actor
- February 8
  - Daisuke Gōri, Japanese voice actor (d. 2010)
  - Nora Miao, Hong Kong actress
- February 10 – Lee Hsien Loong, the 3rd Prime Minister of Singapore
- February 12 – Simon MacCorkindale, English actor (d. 2010)
- February 14 – Nancy Keenan, American president of NARAL
- February 15
  - Nikolai Sorokin, Soviet and Russian actor, theatre director (d. 2013)
  - Tomislav Nikolić, the president of Serbia (since 2012)
- February 17 – Garry Chalk, British voice actor
- February 19 – Amy Tan, American novelist
- February 22 – William Frist, U.S. Senator and heart surgeon
- February 24 – Maxine Chernoff, American poet, novelist, editor
- February 25 – Joey Dunlop, Northern Irish motorcycle racer (d. 2000)

- February 29
    - Gary The Retard, American member of *The Wack Pack* (*The Howard Stern Show*)
    - Sharon Dahlonega Raiford Bush, American television's first female African-American primetime weather anchor

March

Douglas Adams

- March 1 – Martin O'Neill, Northern Irish footballer and manager
- March 2 – Laraine Newman, American comedian (*Saturday Night Live*)
- March 4
    - Scott Hicks, Australian film director
    - Ronn Moss, American actor
    - Umberto Tozzi, Italian singer
- March 7 – Viv Richards, West Indian cricketer
- March 10 – Morgan Tsvangirai, Zimbabwean politician
- March 11
    - Ricardo Martinelli, President of Panama
    - Douglas Adams, English author (*The Hitchhiker's Guide to the Galaxy*) (d. 2001)
- March 13
    - Ágnes Rapai, Hungarian writer

- Wolfgang Rihm, German composer
- March 16 – Philippe Kahn, French-American businessman and inventor
- March 22 – Bob Costas, American sports announcer
- March 23 – Kim Stanley Robinson, American author
- March 25
  - Jung Chang, Chinese-born author and historian
  - Antanas Mockus, Colombian mathematician and politician
- March 27 – Maria Schneider, French actress (d. 2011)
- March 29 – Teofilo Stevenson, Cuban boxer (d. 2012)
- March 30 – Peter Knights, Australian footballer and coach
- March 31
  - Dermot Morgan, Irish actor and comedian (d. 1998)
  - Vanessa del Rio, American actress

April

Steven Seagal

Mary McDonnell

Jean-Paul Gaultier

- April 1
  - Bernard Stiegler, French philosopher
  - Annette O'Toole, American actress
- April 2 – Lennart Fagerlund, Swedish cyclist
- April 4
  - Rosemarie Ackermann, German athlete
  - Gary Moore, Irish musician (d. 2011)
- April 5 – Mitch Pileggi, American actor
- April 6 – Marilu Henner, American actress and author
- April 7 – Nichita Danilov, Romanian writer
- April 10 – Steven Seagal, American actor
- April 11
  - Peter Windsor, British sports reporter
  - Qamar Zaman, Pakistani squash player
- April 12 – Ralph Wiley, American sports journalist (d. 2004)
- April 14 – Mickey O'Sullivan, Irish sportsman
- April 15 – Glenn Shadix, American actor (d. 2010)
- April 17
  - Joe Alaskey, American voice actor (d. 2016)
  - Željko Ražnatović, Serbian mobster and paramilitary leader (d. 2000)
- April 19 – Alexis Arguello, Nicaraguan boxer and politician (d. 2009)

- April 20 – Eric Pickles, British politician
- April 21 – Cheryl Gillan, British politician
- April 22 – Marilyn Chambers, American porn actress (d. 2009)
- April 24 – Jean-Paul Gaultier – French Haute couture and Prêt-à-Porter fashion designer
- April 25 – Ketil Bjørnstad, Norwegian pianist
- April 26 – Spice Williams-Crosby, American actress and stunt performer
- April 27 – George Gervin, American basketball player
- April 28 – Mary McDonnell, American actress

May

Robert Zemeckis

George Strait

Mr T

Anne-Marie David

- May 1 – Michael Thornton, British Member of Parliament for Eastleigh
- May 2
    - Campbell McComas, Australian impersonator and broadcaster
    - Isla St Clair, Scottish singer
- May 3
    - Leonid Khachiyan, Russian-born mathematician
    - Allan Wells, Scottish athlete
- May 4 – Michael Barrymore, British comedian and TV presenter
- May 6
    - Gregg Henry, American actor and musician
    - Michael O'Hare, American actor (d. 2012)

- May 8 – Ronnie Dapo, American child actor
- May 10
  - Roland Kaiser, German singer
  - Manuel Mora Morales, Spanish director and writer
- May 11
  - Shohreh Aghdashloo, Iranian actress
  - Frances Fisher, British-born American actress
  - Mike Lupica, American sports journalist
  - Renaud, French composer
- May 13
  - John Kasich, Governor of Ohio
- May 14
  - Robert Zemeckis, American film director
  - David Byrne, Scottish singer-songwriter (Talking Heads)
- May 15 – Chazz Palminteri, American actor
- May 18
  - Diane Duane, American writer
  - Ryūzaburō Ōtomo, Japanese voice actor
  - George Strait, American country musician
- May 19 – Bert van Marwijk, Dutch football manager
- May 20 – Roger Milla, Cameroonian footballer
- May 21 – Mr. T, African-American actor (*The A-Team*)
- May 23 – Anne-Marie David, French singer, Eurovision Song Contest 1973 winner
- May 24 – Sybil Danning, Austrian actress
- May 26 – David Meece, American Christian musician
- May 28 – Victoria Cunningham, American actress and Playboy Playmate

June

Bronisław Komorowski

Liam Neeson

George Papandreou

John Goodman

- June 4
  - Scott Wesley Brown, American Christian musician
  - Bronisław Komorowski, President of Poland
- June 7
  - Hubert Auriol, French racing driver
  - Liam Neeson, Northern Irish actor
  - Orhan Pamuk, Turkish writer, Nobel Prize winner
- June 9 – Yukihiro Takahashi, Japanese musician and singer (*Yellow Magic Orchestra*)
- June 14 – Pat Summitt, American basketball coach (d. 2016)
- June 16
  - George Papandreou, Greek politician
  - Gino Vannelli, Canadian singer and songwriter
- June 17
  - Sarbjit Singh Chadha, Indian enka singer
  - Mike Milbury, American ice hockey player, coach and executive
- June 18
  - Carol Kane, American actress
  - Isabella Rossellini, Italian model and actress
- June 20
  - John Goodman, American actor
  - Kōichi Mashimo, Japanese anime director
  - Vikram Seth, Indian novelist
- June 21
  - Jeremy Coney, New Zealand cricket captain
  - Marcella Detroit, American singer (Shakespears Sister)
  - Kazi Zulkader Siddiqui, Pakistani businessman, academician
- June 22
  - Graham Greene, Canadian (First Nations) actor

- o Alastair Stewart, British newsreader
- June 24 – Stephen Pusey, British-born artist
- June 25
  - o Péter Erdő, Hungarian cardinal
  - o Tim Finn, New Zealand singer-songwriter
- June 27
  - o Madan Kumar Bhandari, Nepalese politician (d. 1993)
  - o Douglas Unger, American novelist
- June 28 – Pietro Mennea, Italian athlete (d. 2013)
- June 29 – Joe Johnson, English snooker player

July

Dan Aykroyd

Alvaro Uribe

David Hasselhoff

- July 1
  - Dan Aykroyd, Canadian actor and comedian (*Saturday Night Live*)
  - Thomas Boni Yayi, President of Benin
- July 3 – Andy Fraser, English musician (d. 2015)
  - Rohinton Mistry, Indian writer
- July 4
  - Álvaro Uribe, President of Colombia
  - John Waite, English singer and musician
- July 8 – Ahmed Nazif, Prime Minister of Egypt
- July 8 – Knud Arne Jürgensen, Danish music, theater and ballet historian
- July 9 – John Tesh, American composer, musician, and television host (*Entertainment Tonight*)
- July 12
  - Voja Antonić, Serbian inventor and writer
  - Philip Taylor Kramer, American rock musician (d. 1995)
  - Liz Mitchell, Jamaican-born singer of Boney M.
- July 14
  - Bob Casale, American keyboardist (Devo)
  - Franklin Graham, American evangelist and son of Billy Graham

- July 15 – Terry O'Quinn, American actor
- July 16 – Stewart Copeland, American rock musician (*The Police*)
- July 17
  - David Hasselhoff, American actor
  - Billy Sprague, American Christian musician
  - Nicolette Larson, American pop singer (d. 1997)
- July 19 – Allen Collins, American rock musician (*Lynyrd Skynyrd*) (d. 1990)
- July 20 – Keiko Matsuzaka, Japanese actress
- July 24 – Gus Van Sant, American film director
- July 25 – Eduardo Souto de Moura, Portuguese Architect
- July 27 – Hannu-Pekka Hänninen, Finnish sports commentator
- July 31
  - Chris Ahrens, American ice hockey player
  - João Barreiros, Portuguese author

August

Patrick Swayze

Paul Reubens

- August 1 – Zoran Djindjic, Serbian politician (d. 2003)
- August 3 – Osvaldo Ardiles, Argentine footballer
- August 4 – Moya Brennan, Irish singer
- August 5 – Louis Walsh, Irish music producer and reality TV show judge
- August 6 – Wojciech Fortuna, Polish ski jumper
- August 7 – Alexei Sayle, English comedian
- August 8
    - Jostein Gaarder, Norwegian author
    - Robin Quivers, African-American radio personality (*The Howard Stern Show*)
- August 9 – Vicki Morgan, American model (d. 1983)
- August 10 – Daniel Hugh Kelly, American actor
- August 11 – Bob Mothersbaugh, American composer and guitarist (Devo)
- August 13 – Herb Ritts, American photographer (d. 2002)
- August 16 – Reginald VelJohnson, American actor
- August 17 – Guillermo Vilas, Argentine tennis player
- August 18 – Patrick Swayze, American actor and dancer (d. 2009)

Jonathan Frakes

- August 19 – Jonathan Frakes, American actor (*Star Trek: The Next Generation*)
- August 21 – Joe Strummer, British rock musician (*The Clash*) (d. 2002)
- August 24 – Linton Kwesi Johnson, Jamaican-born musician and poet
- August 26
  - Bryon Baltimore, Canadian ice hockey player
  - Michael Jeter, American actor of film, stage, and television (d. 2003)
- August 27 – Paul Reubens, American actor, writer and comedian (*Pee-Wee Herman*)
- August 28 – Rita Dove, American poet (1987 Pulitzer Prize, United States Poet Laureate 1993-95)
- August 28 – Wendelin Wiedeking, German businessman
- August 31 — Lee Hyla, American composer

September

Mickey Rourke

Christopher Reeve

- September 2 – Jimmy Connors, American tennis player
- September 8 – Patrick Prosser, Scottish computer scientist
- September 9 – Angela Cartwright, British-American child actress, photographer and painter
- September 12
  - Sergey Karaganov, Russian political scientist
  - Neil Peart, Canadian rock drummer *(Rush)*
- September 16
  - Fatos Nano, Albanian prime minister
  - Mickey Rourke, American film actor, former boxer
- September 18 – Nile Rodgers, American musician and guitarist
- September 19 – George Warrington, president of Amtrak (1998-2002); executive director of NJ Transit (2002–07) (d. 2007)
- September 20 – Manuel Zelaya, President of Honduras
- September 21 – Anneliese Michel, German Roman Catholic believed possessed by demons (d. 1976)
- September 22 – Bob Goodlatte, U.S. Congressman from Virginia
- September 23
  - Jim Morrison, American baseball player
  - Peter Schrank, Political cartoonist

- September 24
  - Joseph Patrick Kennedy II, politician
  - Mark Sandman, American rock musician and artist (d. 1999)
- September 25
  - Jimmy Garvin, American professional wrestler
  - Christopher Reeve, American actor and activist (d. 2004)
- September 26 – Predrag Miletić, Serbian actor
- September 27
  - Didier Dubois, French mathematician
  - Katie Fforde, British writer
- September 28 – Sylvia Kristel, Dutch actress (d. 2012)
- September 29 – Max Sandlin, American politician
- September 30 – Jack Wild, English actor *(H.R. Pufnstuf)* (d. 2006)

October

Vladimir Putin

Jeff Goldblum

- October 5
  - Clive Barker, British author
  - Harold Faltermeyer, German musician
  - Imran Khan, Pakistani politician
  - Emomali Rahmon, President of Tajikistan
  - Duncan Regehr, Canadian actor
- October 7
  - Mary Badham, American actress
  - Vladimir Putin, President of Russia
  - Richard Walsh, English actor
- October 13
  - Beverly Johnson, African-American model, actress and businesswoman
  - John Lone, Hong Kong actor
- October 14 – Kaija Saariaho, Finnish composer
- October 14 – Nikolai Andrianov, Soviet gymnast (d. 2011)
- October 14 – Rick Aviles, American actor (d. 1995)
- October 16 – Ron Taylor, American actor (d. 2002)
- October 18 – Chuck Lorre, American sitcom creator
- October 22 – Jeff Goldblum, American actor
- October 24 – David Weber, American science fiction and fantasy author
- October 26 – Andrew Motion, English poet

- October 27
  - Topi Sorsakoski, Finnish singer
  - Francis Fukuyama, American political scientist
- October 28 – Annie Potts, American actress

November

Roseanne Barr

David Petraeus

Shigeru Miyamoto

Imran Khan

- November 3
  - Roseanne Barr, American actress and comedian
  - Jim Cummings, American voice actor
  - David Ho, Taiwanese-American AIDS researcher
- November 5
  - Oleh Blokhin, Ukrainian football player and manager
  - Brian Muehl, American puppeteer
  - Bill Walton, American basketball player and commentator
- November 6
  - Michael Cunningham, American writer
  - Christopher Gaze, British voice actor
- November 7 – David Petraeus, American general
- November 8
  - Jan Raas, Dutch professional cyclist
  - Alfre Woodard, African-American actress
- November 13 – Art Malik, Pakistani-born British actor
- November 15 – Randy Savage, American professional wrestler (d. 2011)
- November 16
  - Roger Bisby, English journalist
  - Shigeru Miyamoto, Japanese game designer
- November 17 – Ties Kruize, Dutch field hockey player

- November 24 – Ilja Richter, German actor, voice actor, television presenter, singer and author
- November 25 – Imran Khan, Pakistani cricketer and politician
- November 27 – Buddy Rose, American professional wrestler (d. 2009)
- November 28 – S. Epatha Merkerson, African-American actress
- November 30 – Keith Giffen, American comic book writer and artist

December

Allan Simonsen

- December 2 – Peter Kingsbery, American singer-songwriter (Cock Robin)
- December 3 – Bruno Jonas, German Kabarett artist and actor
- December 6
  - Chuck Baker, American Major League Baseball player
  - Nicolas Bréhal, French novelist and literary critic
  - Charles Bronson, English criminal (has been referred to as the "most violent prisoner in Britain")
  - Edward Etzel, American Olympic Champion
  - Joe Harris, American football linebacker
  - Christian Kulik, Polish football player

- o Craig Newmark, American businessman, founded Craigslist
- o Shio Satō, Japanese manga artist
- o Jeff Schneider, American Major League Baseball pitcher
- o David L. Spector, American cell and molecular biologist
- December 9 – Michael Dorn, African-American actor (*Star Trek: The Next Generation*)
- December 12
  - o Harbance Singh (Herb) Dhaliwal, Canadian politician
  - o Sarah Douglas, English actress
- December 13
  - o Greg Greenway, American Singer-Songwriter
  - o Karl Howman, English actor
- December 15
  - o Julie Taymor, American film, theater, and opera director and costume designer
  - o Hwang Woo-suk, South Korean biomedical scientist
  - o Allan Simonsen, Danish footballer and coach
- December 16 – Joel Garner, West Indian cricketer
- December 20 – Jenny Agutter, English actress
- December 26
  - o Jon Glover, British actor
  - o Riki Sorsa, Finnish singer (d. 2016)
- December 27
  - o Jay Hill, Canadian politician
  - o David Knopfler, British musician
- December 28
  - o Arun Jaitley, Indian politician
  - o Hemant Shesh, Indian Hindi Writer
- December 30 – June Anderson, American soprano

Date unknown

- Idriss Déby Itno, President of Chad

Deaths

January

King George VI

- January 5 – Hristo Tatarchev, Bulgarian revolutionary (b. 1869)
- January 11 – Jean de Lattre de Tassigny, French general, posthumous Marshal of France (b. 1889)
- January 18 – Curly Howard, American actor and comedian (*The Three Stooges*) (b. 1903)
- January 25 – Polly Moran, American actress (b. 1883)
- January 27 – Fannie Ward, American actress (b. 1872)

February

- February 2 – Charles de Rochefort, French actor (b. 1879)
- February 3 – Harold L. Ickes, United States Secretary of the Interior (b. 1874)

- February 6 – King George VI of the United Kingdom (b. 1895)
- February 7
  - Philip G. Epstein, American screenwriter (b. 1909)
  - Pete Henry, American football player (Canton Bulldogs) and a member of the Pro Football Hall of Fame (b. 1897)
- February 9 – Arthur Hayes-Sadler, British admiral (b. 1865)
- February 19 – Knut Hamsun, Norwegian author, Nobel Prize laureate (b. 1859)

March

- March 1 – Gregory La Cava, American film director (b. 1892)
- March 5 – Charles Scott Sherrington, English physiologist, Nobel Prize laureate (b. 1857)
- March 7 – Paramahansa Yogananda, Indian guru (b. 1893)
- March 9 – Alexandra Kollontai, Russian revolutionary (b. 1872)
- March 12 – Hugh Herbert, American actor and comedian (b. 1887)
- March 22
  - Uncle Dave Macon, American musician (b. 1870)
  - Don Stephen Senanayake, Ceylonese (Sri Lankan) Prime Minister (b. 1884)
- March 26 – J.P. McGowan, Australian actor and director (b. 1880)
- March 28 – Sir Fraser Russell, Governor of Southern Rhodesia (b. 1876)
- March 31
  - Walter Schellenberg, German Nazi intelligence official (b. 1910)

- ○ Roland West, American film director (b. 1885)
- ○ Wallace H. White, Jr., U.S. Senator from Maine (b. 1877)

April

- April 1 – Ferenc Molnár, Hungarian novelist and dramatist (b. 1878)
- April 3 – Miina Sillanpää, Finnish politician (b. 1866)
- April 5 – Charles Collett, British chief mechanical engineer (*Great Western Railway*) (b. 1871)
- April 8 – Tadeusz Estreicher, cryogenics pioneer (b. 1871)
- April 15 – Viktor Chernov, Russian revolutionary, leader of the Russian Socialist Revolutionary Party (b. 1873)
- April 21
    - ○ Leslie Banks, English actor (b. 1890)
    - ○ Sir Stafford Cripps, British Labour politician, former Chancellor of the Exchequer (b. 1889)
- April 23 – Julius Freed, American inventor and banker (b. 1887)

May

Maria Montessori

- May 6 – Maria Montessori, Italian educator (b. 1870)
- May 8 – William Fox, Austro-Hungarian-born film producer (b. 1879)
- May 9 – Canada Lee, American actor (b. 1907)

- May 10 – Clark L. Hull, American psychologist (b. 1884)
- May 15 – Albert Bassermann, German actor (b. 1867)
- May 21 – John Garfield, American actor (b. 1913)

June

- June 1
  - John Dewey, American philosopher (b. 1859)
  - Malcolm St. Clair, American filmmaker (b. 1897)
- June 2 – Naum Torbov, Bulgarian architect (b. 1880)
- June 13 – Emma Eames, American soprano (b. 1865)
- June 17 – Krystyna Skarbek (aka Christine Granville), Polish-born British SOE operative during World War II (b. 1908)
  - Jack Parsons, American rocket engineer (b. 1914)
- June 19 – Heinrich Schlusnus, German baritone (b. 1888)
- June 27 – Elmo Lincoln, American actor (b. 1889)

July

Eva Perón

- July 4 – Walter Long, American character actor (b. 1879)
- July 5 – Alison Skipworth, English actress (b. 1863)

- July 10 – Rued Langgaard, Danish composer and organist (b. 1893)
- July 21 – Pedro Lascuráin, 34th President of Mexico
- July 26 – Eva Perón, Argentine political leader, and First Lady to and partner in power of President Juan Perón (b. 1919)

August

- August 1 – Andrew Higgins, American boatbuilder and industrialist. (b. 1886)
- August 2 – J. Farrell MacDonald, American actor and director (b. 1875)
- August 5 – Sameera Moussa, Egyptian nuclear scientist (b. 1917)
- August 11 – Dave Sands, Australian boxer (b. 1926)
- August 18 – Ralph Byrd, American actor (b. 1909)
- August 29 – Anton Piëch, Austrian lawyer, son-in-law of Ferdinand Porsche (b. 1894)
- August 30 – Arky Vaughan, American baseball player (Pittsburgh Pirates) and a member of the MLB Hall of Fame (b. 1912)

September

- September 6 – Gertrude Lawrence, English actress (b. 1898)
- September 9 – Jonas H. Ingram, American admiral (b. 1886)
- September 16 – Hugo Raudsepp, Estonian playwright (b. 1883)
- September 22 – Kaarlo Juho Ståhlberg, 1st President of Finland (b. 1865)
- September 23 – Ray Mala, Native American actor (b. 1906)

- September 26 – George Santayana, Spanish-born writer (b. 1863)
- September 30 – Viscount Waldorf Astor, American-born businessman and politician (b. 1879)

October

- October 11 – Jack Conway, American film producer and director (b. 1887)
- October 17 – Julia Dean, stage and screen actress (b. 1878)
- October 20 – Basil Radford, English actor (b. 1897)
- October 22 – Ernst Rüdin, Swiss psychiatrist, geneticist, and eugenicist (b. 1874)
- October 23 – Susan Peters, American actress (b. 1921)
- October 26 – Hattie McDaniel, American actress (b. 1895)
- October 28 – Billy Hughes, 7th Prime Minister of Australia (b. 1862)

November

- November 1 – Dixie Lee, American singer (b. 1911)
- November 2 – Mehmet Esat Bülkat, Ottoman general (b. 1862)
- November 3 – Louis Verneuil, French playwright, screenwriter (b. 1893)
- November 8
  - Harold Innis, Canadian communications scholar (b. 1894)
  - Hugh Prosser, American actor (b. 1900)
- November 9 – Chaim Weizmann, Jewish biochemist and first President of Israel (b. 1874)
- November 18 – Paul Eluard, French poet (b. 1895)

- November 20 – Benedetto Croce, Italian critic, philosopher, and politician (b. 1866)
- November 21
  - Henriette Roland Holst, Dutch poet and socialist (b. 1869)
  - William D. Upshaw, American temperance movement leader (b. 1866)
- November 26 – Sven Hedin, Swedish explorer, geographer and geopolitician (b. 1865)
- November 28 – Elena of Montenegro, Queen of Italy, consort of Victor Emmanuel III (b. 1869)

December

- December 1 – Vittorio Emanuele Orlando, 23rd Prime Minister of Italy (b. 1860)
- December 4 – Karen Horney, German psychoanalyst (b. 1885)
- December 8 – Charles Lightoller, British merchant marine officer, second officer of RMS *Titanic* (b. 1874)
- December 12 – Bedrich Hrozný, Czech orientalist and linguist (b. 1879)
- December 14 – Fartein Valen, Norwegian composer (b. 1887)
- December 18 – Ernst Stromer, German paleontologist (b. 1871)
- December 19 – Pehr G. Holmes, American politician (b. 1881)
- December 27 – Henri Winkelman, Dutch general (b. 1876)
- December 28
  - Alexandrine of Mecklenburg-Schwerin, Queen consort of Christian X of Denmark (b. 1879)
  - Fletcher Henderson, American musician (b. 1897)

- December 30 – Luke McNamee, American admiral and Governor of Guam (b. 1871)

Date unknown

- K. Kanagaratnam, Ceylon Tamil civil servant and politician (b. 1892)

Nobel Prizes

- Physics – Felix Bloch, Edward Mills Purcell
- Chemistry – Archer John Porter Martin, Richard Laurence Millington Synge
- Medicine – Selman Abraham Waksman
- Literature – François Mauriac
- Peace – Albert Schweitzer

In the News

Albert Einstein refuses Presidency of Israel.

Thick smog in London on December 4th , England causes 4,000 fatalities.

Elizabeth II becomes Queen upon the death of her father George VI.

Three Trains crash at Harrow in North London.

South African Police Arrest Nelson Mandella.

Britain announces it has Atomic Bomb.

Rocky Marciano becomes world heavyweight champion after knocking out Jersey Joe Walcott.

The Summer Olympics are held in July in Helsinki, Finland.

Popular Films - The African Queen, Greatest Show on Earth, The Quiet man, Singin' in the Rain.

The worlds first passenger jet is produced in UK (The Comet) and flies for the first time on May 2nd.